SPACE EXPLORATION

HUMAN MISSIONS
TO OUTER SPACE

Laurie Calkhoven

Children's Press®
An imprint of Scholastic Inc.

Content Consultant
Roger D. Launius, PhD
Former Chief Historian, NASA

Library of Congress Cataloging-in-Publication Data

Names: Calkhoven, Laurie, author.

Title: Human missions to Outer Space/Laurie Calkhoven.

Other titles: True book.

Description: First edition. | New York: Children's Press, an imprint of Scholastic, Inc., 2022. | Series: A true book | Includes bibliographical references and index. | Audience: Ages 8–10. | Audience: Grades 4–6. | Summary: "A new set of True Books on Space Exploration"—Provided by publisher.

Identifiers: LCCN 2021041621 (print) | LCCN 2021041622 (ebook) | ISBN 9781338825916 (library binding) | ISBN 9781338825923 (paperback) | ISBN 9781338825930 (ebook)

Subjects: LCSH: Manned space flight—Juvenile literature. | Outer space—Exploration—Juvenile literature. | BISAC: JUVENILE NONFICTION / Technology / Aeronautics, Astronautics & Space Science | JUVENILE NONFICTION / General

Classification: LCC TL793 .C335 2022 (print) | LCC TL793 (ebook) | DDC 629.45—dc23

LC record available at https://lccn.loc.gov/2021041621

LC ebook record available at https://lccn.loc.gov/2021041622

10 9 8 7 6 5 4 3 2   23 24 25 26

Printed in the U.S.A. 113
First edition, 2022

Design by Kathleen Petelinsek
Series produced by Spooky Cheetah Press

Front cover: NASA astronaut Bruce McCandless II as seen from the space shuttle Challenger

Back cover: Gemini 6 as seen from the window of Gemini 7

Find the Truth!

Everything you are about to read is true *except* for one of the sentences on this page.

Which one is **TRUE**?

T or F   Astronauts can't talk to anyone on Earth while they are in space.

T or F   Astronauts drove a car on the moon.

Find the answers in this book.

What's in This Book?

The **BIG** Truth

Ham was the
first chimpanzee
in space.

Mission Support

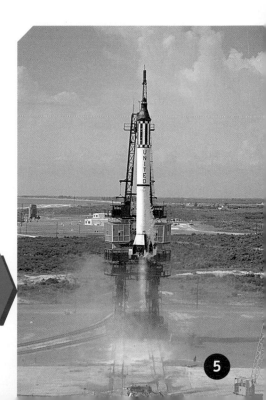

The first spacewalk

3 A New Way to Fly

4 The Future of Space Exploration

The first American blasted into space on May 5, 1961.

What's Out There?

Humans probably started **dreaming about exploring the universe** from the first time they looked up at the **stars twinkling** in the night sky. But it wasn't until 60 years ago that **rockets made it possible** for us to escape Earth's **gravity** and travel beyond our **atmosphere**. The first trips to outer space were uncrewed. But later on, many brave men and women dared to strap themselves into those **powerful rockets** to be propelled into Earth's **orbit.** A few journeyed as far away as the moon. Each of those missions was meaningful. They all brought back information that made **further discoveries possible** for those who followed. Read on to learn about the daring and exciting journeys to outer space that have brought us closer to **unlocking the mysteries of the universe.**

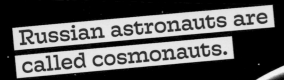

Russian astronauts are called cosmonauts.

It took cosmonaut Yuri Gagarin 108 minutes to complete one orbit of Earth in this capsule.

The Dawn of the Space Age

After World War II ended in 1949, the United States was one of the world's superpowers. The Soviet Union (which included today's Russia) was another. Each country wanted to be the first to explore space. The Soviet Union won the first leg of the space race by sending the first **satellite**, Sputnik, into orbit on October 4, 1957. The world was shocked again, on April 12, 1961, when Soviet cosmonaut Yuri Gagarin became the first human in space.

The Race Heats Up

The United States set its sights on being first to send a person to the moon. But there was a lot to be learned before any American could make that trip.

The National Aeronautics and Space Administration (NASA), which had been established in 1958, oversees U.S. space exploration. Its first space program was Project Mercury. It had three goals: to send an American into orbit around Earth, bring the astronaut and craft home safely, and study the effects of space on the human body.

Jerrie Cobb stands next to a Mercury capsule. Cobb trained like the male astronauts but, because women were not accepted into the program, she didn't get to go into space.

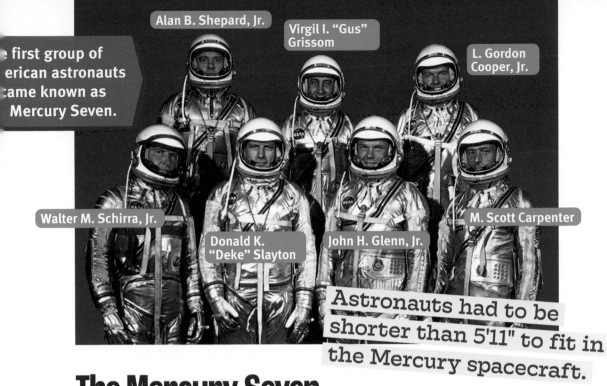

Alan B. Shepard, Jr.

Virgil I. "Gus" Grissom

L. Gordon Cooper, Jr.

first group of erican astronauts came known as Mercury Seven.

Walter M. Schirra, Jr.

Donald K. "Deke" Slayton

John H. Glenn, Jr.

M. Scott Carpenter

Astronauts had to be shorter than 5'11" to fit in the Mercury spacecraft.

The Mercury Seven

Seven male military officers were chosen to be the first group of astronauts. All of them were pilots with more than 1,500 hours of flying time. They had to pass a series of challenging physical and mental tests. The astronauts also had to be very daring.

Space exploration was a brand-new science. Many early rockets blew up on the launchpad. Yet these seven brave heroes volunteered to be blasted into space.

Alan B. Shepard's flight lasted 15 minutes and 28 seconds.

The Mercury craft blasted off on a Redstone rocket. The rocket was originally designed as a missile for the U.S. military.

Mercury Blasts Off!

The Mercury spacecraft had room for just one astronaut. On May 5, 1961, less than a month after Yuri Gagarin's flight, that seat was taken by Alan B. Shepard. He became the first American in space during a **suborbital** flight aboard Freedom 7.

Eight months later, John Glenn became the first American to orbit Earth. He circled the planet three times aboard the spacecraft Friendship 7.

In total, six successful Mercury missions paved the way for NASA'S next space program—Project Gemini.

Can Fish Swim and Bees Fly in Space?

In 1958, a Russian dog named Laika had been sent into orbit, becoming the first animal in space. Since then, other animals have taken flight, including several primates, especially monkeys and chimpanzees. Astronauts have also studied all kinds of other animals in space, including fish and honeybees. Like the astronauts themselves, these animals had to adapt to **microgravity**. At first, the fish swam in loops instead of in straight lines as they do on Earth, but they soon adapted to space. Likewise, after a few days of confusion, the honeybees were finally able to build a honeycomb!

Ham, a chimpanzee, flew in a Mercury spacecraft three months before Alan Shepard's flight.

This photo of Gemini 6 was taken through the window of Gemini 7.

Project Gemini: A Bridge to the Moon

Ten crewed Gemini missions were flown from 1965 to 1966. Project Gemini accomplished three goals: The astronauts were able to maneuver, **rendezvous,** and dock with another spacecraft. They practiced working outside a spacecraft. And NASA learned what happens to the human body during long-duration spaceflight. The 10 Gemini missions prepared the way for the Apollo missions to come.

The First Space Walk

Before astronauts could land on the moon, NASA had to find a way to enable them to survive in space—outside a spacecraft. Spacewalkers face temperatures as cold as −250 degrees Fahrenheit (−157 degrees Celsius) and as hot as 250°F (121°C) in sunlight. NASA had to design a spacesuit that would protect astronauts from the extreme temperatures in space. The suit also needed to provide oxygen for the astronauts to breathe and water to drink.

On June 3, 1965, during the Gemini 4 mission, astronaut Ed White put on one of those spacesuits and became the first American to step out of a craft and into the cold, dark reaches of space.

Astronauts are weightless in space. If White had not been tethered to his spacecraft, he would have floated away!

Ed White was attached to the spacecraft by a 25-foot tether during his 23-minute spacewalk.

Every Apollo mission that landed on the moon left an American flag. They are all still there.

Astronauts Buzz Aldrin (pictured) and Neil Armstrong planted an American flag on the moon.

To the Moon!

To land astronauts on the moon and bring them home safely, NASA needed its most powerful rocket to date, the Saturn V. It also needed its most sophisticated spacecraft yet: Apollo.

The Apollo spacecraft had three parts. The astronauts would live and work in the Command **Module**. The Service Module would carry equipment. And the **Lunar** Module would fly two astronauts to the moon's surface and then return them to the Command Module.

These are the three astronauts who lost their lives during the first Apollo mission (left to right): Gus Grissom, Ed White, and Roger Chaffee.

Tragedy and Triumph

Sadly, in January 1967, a tragedy took place in which three astronauts died while training for the first Apollo mission. The investigation that followed the accident led NASA to make changes in the Apollo capsule that made it safer for future missions.

In October 1968, Apollo 7 tested the spacecraft and procedures. Apollo 8 was the first crewed spacecraft to orbit the moon. After two more missions, it was time to land humans on our satellite.

One Giant Leap for Mankind

Apollo 11 reached the moon on July 20, 1969. The Lunar Module split apart from the Command Module and landed on the moon's surface. Michael Collins orbited in the command module while Neil Armstrong and Edwin "Buzz" Aldrin got ready to become the first people to walk on the moon.

As Armstrong stepped out onto the surface of the moon, he said these famous words: "That's one small step for man. One giant leap for mankind."

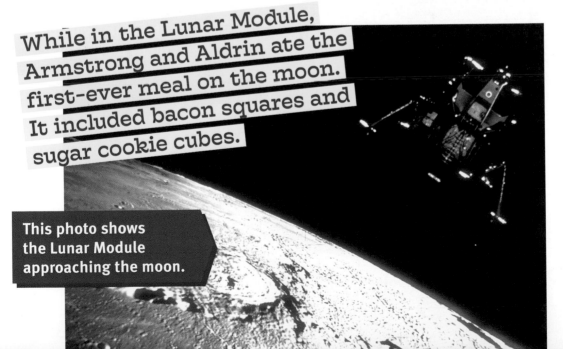

While in the Lunar Module, Armstrong and Aldrin ate the first-ever meal on the moon. It included bacon squares and sugar cookie cubes.

This photo shows the Lunar Module approaching the moon.

Splashdown!

Armstrong and Aldrin spent about two hours on the moon's surface gathering rocks and dust to take home. Then they powered up the Lunar Module's rocket to rendezvous with the Command Module, which was orbiting the moon. Finally, the spacecraft hurtled back toward home. It splashed down in the Pacific Ocean almost three days after leaving the moon's orbit.

The astronauts were transferred from the capsule to a life raft. Then they were picked up by a helicopter.

Astronauts drove the Lunar Rover around on the moon to explore even more of the moon's surface.

Apollos 7, 8, 9, and 10 orbited Earth or the moon. Apollos 11, 12, 14, 15, 16, and 17 landed on the moon.

Apollo's Last Mission

There were 11 Apollo flights from 1968 to 1972. On the last three, the Lunar Module carried a vehicle called a Lunar Rover. The Apollo 17 mission, which launched in December 1972, was the last to send humans to the moon. The enormous cost of crewed lunar missions led NASA to end the Apollo program.

Mission Support

Astronauts might be by themselves inside the spacecraft, but they do not take the trip to outer space alone. A huge team of people on Earth, the Mission Control Center (MCC), works to develop and support every mission. MCC also keeps the astronauts safe. Learn more about how this important team works!

Meet the Team

A flight director oversees every mission to outer space with the help of scientists, engineers, and even a flight surgeon, who keeps an eye on the astronauts' health. Thousands of people support every space mission! All of them are key to the success of NASA's space program.

Apollo MCC

Constant Contact

MCC uses satellites to stay in constant contact with the astronauts throughout the mission, ready to help them make life-or-death decisions. When there was an explosion on Apollo 13, MCC worked through the night to design an air filter the astronauts could build from spare parts. It saved their lives!

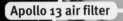
Apollo 13 air filter

Students in MCC, 2013

Special Guests

In June 2010, NASA debuted the Student Spaceflight Experiments Program (SSEP), a competition that allows American students to design an experiment to be conducted on the International Space Station. Winning teams get to join the support team at MCC to watch their projects blast off!

The shuttles lifted off like rockets and returned to Earth like airplanes.

All space shuttles launched from the Kennedy Space Center in Florida.

CHAPTER

A New Way to Fly

After Apollo, NASA set its sights on a new challenge. Before, rockets and spacecraft could be used only once. NASA wanted to develop a reusable craft, which would be more affordable. The result was the space shuttle fleet.

From 1981 to 2011, the space shuttle made space travel possible for more people than ever before.

A Three-Part System

Each shuttle had three parts. A pair of booster rockets provided the power needed to leave Earth's atmosphere. The orbiter carried the crew and the cargo. A fuel tank carried fuel for the orbiter's engines.

It took the shuttle only 10 minutes to reach space. Within two minutes of liftoff, the booster rockets dropped off and landed in the ocean, to be picked up by a NASA ship. Six minutes later, the orbiter's fuel tanks dropped off and burned up on **reentry** into Earth's atmosphere. Two minutes after that, the orbiter reached orbit.

Disasters in Space

Spaceflight is risky, and astronauts sometimes don't come home safely. The space shuttle program had two tragic disasters, which cost the lives of 14 astronauts.

At the time of the Challenger shuttle liftoff, on January 28, 1986, Florida had a cold snap that froze two rubber rings on one of the shuttle's rocket boosters. Just 73 seconds into the launch, the shuttle broke apart, killing all seven crew members on board.

Space shuttle Columbia was heading home on February 1, 2003, after 16 days in space, when the orbiter broke apart on reentry. NASA later learned that a piece of foam had broken loose during liftoff and damaged the orbiter's left wing. Hot gases entered the wing when the shuttle returned to Earth's atmosphere, and the aircraft disintegrated, killing all seven astronauts.

The Columbia crew

The Challenger crew

A Busy Fleet

The space shuttles operated from 1981 through 2011. During that time, NASA's space shuttle fleet flew 135 missions!

The world's first reusable spacecraft carried humans into orbit and enabled scientific experiments. The shuttle also made possible the building of the International Space Station,

Milestones in Human Missions to Outer Space

APRIL 12, 1961
Soviet cosmonaut Yuri Gagarin becomes the first human in space.

FEBRUARY 20, 1962
Astronaut John Glenn is the first American to orbit Earth.

JUNE 16, 1963
Soviet cosmonaut Valentina Tereshkova becomes the first woman in space. She orbits Earth 48 times in nearly 71 hours.

JULY 20, 1969
U.S. astronauts Neil Armstrong and Buzz Aldrin walk on the moon.

a high-flying laboratory where astronauts from many countries live, work, and conduct experiments. Astronauts used the shuttle as a base to walk in space and to connect with other spacecraft.

The shuttle and the thousands of people who worked in the shuttle program pushed the bounds of discovery, helping NASA get ready for even greater exploration in the future. All together, the shuttle fleet spent 1,334 days in space.

AUGUST 30, 1983
Guion "Guy" Bluford becomes the first Black person to fly in space.

NOVEMBER 2, 2000
A crew boards the International Space Station for the very first time.

JULY 21, 2011
Space shuttle Atlantis safely completes the program's final mission.

DECEMBER 9, 2020
NASA announces the names of the 18 astronauts who will form the Artemis Team to travel back to the moon and beyond.

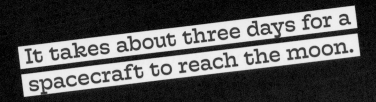

It takes about three days for a spacecraft to reach the moon.

This artwork shows crews working on the moon.

The Future of Space Exploration

The final lunar landing mission took place in 1972. Since then, no human has been farther than a few hundred miles from Earth. That's probably going to change in the next decades. In 2020, NASA revealed plans to land the first woman and the first person of color on the moon. These astronauts will be part of the crew of NASA's new lunar exploration program: Artemis.

A New Rocket for a New Spacecraft

The SLS rocket is the most powerful rocket ever built. It will launch the spacecraft Orion on its moon mission. The craft will provide the life support systems that the four-member crew will need during lunar orbit and return to Earth.

A New Suit for a New Mission

The spacesuit being developed for Artemis missions is called the Exploration Extravehicular Mobility Unit (xEMU). This is one version of the suit that is being tested.

HELMET WITH VISOR protects the eyes and face from the sun's damaging rays. It also has microphones for communication.

LIFE SUPPORT SYSTEM provides oxygen and temperature control and has other features that keep the astronaut safe.

SHOULDER AND WAIST sections are adjustable to fit different body sizes and types.

CONTROL PANEL operates the life support system.

SPACESUIT MATERIAL is more flexible than existing suits, which will make it easier for the astronauts to move around.

The Lunar South Pole

The first Artemis mission will not carry a crew on its trip around the moon. It will simply test the spacecraft. Artemis 2 will orbit the moon with a crew and return to Earth without landing on the moon. On the Artemis 3 mission, two astronauts may visit an area of the moon where no humans have ever gone: the lunar south pole.

Sea of Tranquility

Ocean of Storms

The lunar south pole contains frozen water.

South Pole

The plan is for Artemis 3 to dock with the Lunar Gateway and stay in space for 30 days.

This is a concept illustration of Gateway orbiting the moon.

Gateway to the Moon

Artemis astronauts won't be living on the moon. For future missions, Orion will connect with a small space station, the Lunar Gateway, that will orbit the moon. It will be a hub for scientific experiments, a docking port for spacecraft carrying astronauts and cargo, and a launch port for expeditions even farther into space.

On the Gateway, astronauts will learn how to live and work in **deep space**.

Unraveling the Moon's Mysteries

Scientists have known since the 1990s that there is water in the moon's dark, cold areas, like its south pole. Water is vital for human survival in space. Can the moon's water be used for drinking? Can enough of it be separated into its components, hydrogen and oxygen, to create rocket fuel and air for breathing?

Answering those questions may make it possible to travel deeper into the solar system.

NASA wants to use the moon as a science platform. From there, we can look back at the Earth, study the sun, and get ready for the next giant leap in space exploration—sending astronauts to Mars.

This concept illustration shows astronauts working on the moon.

Earth and Mars orbit the sun at different speeds. Mars-bound spacecraft will have to chase Mars around the sun before landing.

The Future of Humans in Space

NASA plans to send astronauts to the Red Planet and back again as early as the 2030s. It would take about seven months for them to reach Mars.

Before humans land on Mars, NASA will send life support systems ahead of time and make sure they land safely. These include systems that are necessary to the astronauts' survival, like oxygen for them to breathe and filters to absorb dangerous

This is a concept illustration of homes on Mars.

carbon dioxide. Humans will also need water to drink, food to eat, and a way to manage waste like trash and urine millions of miles away from home.

With new discoveries in the science of spaceflight and brave astronauts stepping up to explore the solar system, space is opening up like never before. The future of space exploration is limitless.

Taste in Space

Scientists at NASA conduct experiments to see how space travel affects humans. One study tested an astronaut's sense of taste on the ground and then again soon after arriving in space. Study the results, and then answer the questions that follow.

An astronaut aboard the International Space Station gets ready to eat his burrito dinner. It is floating around him!

Astronaut Taste Data

Food Tasted	Ground Tasting			Space Tasting		
	Identified? Yes/No (thought to be)	Flavor (salty, sweet, etc.)	Intensity (0=none, 10= max)	Identified? Yes/No	Flavor (salty, sweet, etc.)	Intensity (0=none, 10= max)
Applesauce	Y	Sweet	6	Y	Sweet and fruity	4
Cream of Mushroom Soup	(Chicken soup)	Salty	6	N	Very salty	7
Blueberry/ Raspberry Yogurt	N	Hard to tell, slightly sweet	4	N	Smooth and bland	2
Chocolate Breakfast Drink	Y	Thick chocolate due to sweetness	6	Y	Full-bodied and sweet	6
Black Coffee	(Green tea)	A sharp taste	10	N	Sharp and bitter, very unpleasant	8
Orange Juice	(Citrus juice)	Tart	7	N	Guessed it as grapefruit juice	4

Source: https://www.nasa.gov/sites/default/files/files/Taste-in-space-TLA-FINAL.pdf

Analyze It!

1 Where did the astronaut have a better idea of what food was being tasted—on the ground or in space?

2 Were tastes more intense on Earth or in space?

3 Overall, were the space tastings more or less enjoyable than the ground tastings?

4 Do you use any condiments on your food at home? Which ones and why? Why do you think most astronauts add condiments to their food in space?

ANSWERS: 1. On the ground, even though sometimes the astronaut did not guess the flavor of the item exactly. 2. On Earth. 3. Less enjoyable. 4. Astronauts typically use condiments to add extra flavor to their food in space.

Build a Rocket

When a rocket burns fuel, it creates a powerful jet of hot gas. The force of the gas pushing down thrusts the rocket upward. You can mimic that process with this activity.

Materials

Bicycle pump with needle adapter

Cork

Empty plastic bottle

Duct tape or hot glue

Construction paper nose cone

Four cardboard fins

Water

Safety glasses

⚠ Directions

ASK AN ADULT FOR HELP

1 Push the needle adapter all the way through the cork. If it doesn't go all the way through, ask an adult to trim the cork. Place the cork with the adaptor to the side.

2 Using duct tape or hot glue, attach the nose cone to the bottom of the bottle. Attach the fins to the sides of the bottle, near the mouth. The fins will provide a stable base for your rocket to launch, so place them carefully.

3 Add water to the bottle until it is 1/4 full. Push the cork into the mouth as tightly as you can. Take your rocket outside. Connect the needle adapter to the pump and place your rocket on a flat surface.

! ASK AN ADULT FOR HELP

Explain It!

Using what you learned in this book, can you explain how the rocket was able to launch?

4 Put on the safety glasses. Standing as far from the rocket as possible, pump air into the rocket until it launches.

True Statistics

Average distance from Earth to the moon: 238,855 miles (384,400 km)

Average distance from Earth to Mars: 140 million miles (225 million km)

Gravity of the moon compared to Earth: 16% (about one-sixth the gravity of Earth)

Gravity of Mars compared to Earth: 38%

Number of Apollo missions that landed on the moon: 6

Number of astronauts who have walked on the moon: 12

Total miles traveled by the space shuttles: 537,114,016 through 135 flights

Estimated time each of the Apollo 11 astronauts spent training in simulators on Earth before their moon mission: 2,000 hours

Did you find the truth?

 F Astronauts can't talk to anyone on Earth while they are in space.

 T Astronauts drove a car on the moon.

Resources

Other books in this series:

 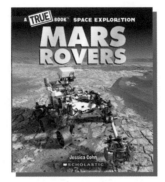 

You can also look at:

Floca, Brian. *Moonshot: The Flight of Apollo 11*. New York: Atheneum Books for Young Readers, 2019.

Galat, Joan Marie. *Absolute Expert: Space*. Washington, D.C.: National Geographic Kids Books, 2020.

Jenkins, Martin. *Exploring Space: From Galileo to the Mars Rover and Beyond*. Somerville, MA: Candlewick Press, 2017.

Olson, Tod. *Lost in Outer Space: The Incredible Journey of Apollo 13*. New York: Scholastic, 2017.

Glossary

atmosphere (AT-muhs-feer) the mixture of gases that surrounds a planet

deep space (deep spays) space far beyond Earth's atmosphere and especially that part outside the Earth-moon system

gravity (GRAV-i-tee) the force that pulls things toward the center of the earth and keeps them from floating away

lunar (LOO-nur) of or having to do with the moon

microgravity (mye-kroh-GRAV-i-tee) a condition in space when the pull of gravity is not very strong

module (MAH-jool) a separate unit that can be joined to others to make things, such as two parts of a spaceship

orbit (OR-bit) the curved path followed by a moon, planet, or satellite as it circles a planet or the sun

reentry (ree-EN-tree) the return of a spacecraft to Earth's atmosphere

rendezvous (RAHN-day-voo) the process of bringing two spacecraft together

satellite (SAT-uh-lite) a spacecraft, a moon, or another heavenly body that travels in an orbit around a larger heavenly body

suborbital (sub-OR-bit-al) involving less than a complete orbit of Earth or the moon

Index

Page numbers in **bold** indicate illustrations.

About the Author

Laurie Calkhoven was 10 years old when Neil Armstrong and Buzz Aldrin landed on the moon. She got to stay up extra late with her sisters and her cousins to watch the event on television. Today, she is the author of more than 50 books for young readers and dreams of one day living in the Artemis Base Camp.